CONTEMPORARY WRITERS IN CHRISTIAN PERSPECTIVE
EDITED BY RODERICK JELLEMA

William Golding

A CRITICAL ESSAY
BY PAUL ELMEN

WILLIAM B. EERDMANS/PUBLISHER

CONTENTS

Fabulous Artificer

William Golding once replied to a literary magazine's question-naire that he was "a citizen, a novelist and a schoolmaster." Writers invariably reply archly to questions which threaten them by means of simple categories; but in this case the answer is informative. Golding is a citizen, in the ancient Greek sense of the word; and he obviously is a novelist, one of the most distinguished writing today; and he is in a deeper sense than he realizes a schoolmaster. Perhaps the better order would be to say that he is a novelist who feels deeply his responsibility to the human estate, and that he recognizes this duty by serving as a teacher. Whether he knows it or not he has a schoolmaster's distaste for mischief, and there hangs over each of the books a faint aroma of chalk.

This preoccupation with morality gives Golding a solemnity which is not widely shared by contemporary novelists. His themes have a Miltonic scope, and meet Matthew Arnold's requirement of high seriousness. "I am very serious," he once replied to a questioner. "I believe that man suffers from an appalling ignorance of his own nature. I produce my own view, in the belief that it may be something like the truth. I am fully engaged to the human dilemma." His basic humility prevents him from identifying his view of truth with the truth itself, but he does not deny himself the hope that such coherence as he discovers is not his own creation but is part of the stuff of reality.

His biography falls into two major parts, divided by World War II. Born in 1911 in a Cornish village, he was educated at Marlborough Grammar School, and went from there to

Brasenose College, Oxford, where he read English. Graduating in 1953, he became a teacher in Bishop Wordsworth's School, Salisbury. He was married in 1939. At first he wrote poetry and had one volume of verse published. In 1940 he joined the Royal Navy, and during the next five years he saw considerable combat including the sinking of the *Bismarck* and the D-Day landings. He left the Navy at the end of the war and resumed his teaching at Bishop Wordsworth's School, but a profound change had occurred in his philosophy of life. Before the war he had been on the whole optimistic about the human condition, placing his faith in a kind of progressive enlightenment which could be achieved by rational effort. But after the war he recognized the radical evil in human nature, and saw that the conventions of society masked a deeper alienation which waited to erupt. To this period belong the early works: *Lord of the Flies* (1955), *The Inheritors* (1955), *Pincher Martin* (1956), *The Brass Butterfly* (1958), *Free Fall* (1960), and many short stories and travel articles. He resigned from his teaching position in 1962, and has spent his time since then travelling and lecturing, teaching, writing, and sailing. *The Spire* was written in 1964, and a collection of essays and fugitive pieces appeared in 1966 under the title *The Hot Gates*.

But the circumstances of a writer's life are only of interest if they cast light upon the things he wrote. The biography of a realist is perhaps of greater importance, since he derives his themes from the stuff of his own experience. But Golding is not a realist, if by that term is meant a writer who studies experience without predicting what he will find. He never begins a novel as a scientist conducts an experiment, sitting down, as Huxley said, before the facts like a little child. He begins with an abstract idea—such as the presence of evil beneath the civilized surface *(Lord of the Flies),* or the loss of innocence in a boy *(Free Fall)*, or the loss of innocence in the race *(The Inheritors)*—and invents a narrative which will embody the truth he has in mind.

For this reason he has been called a fabulist. Writing in the

Kenyon Review in the autumn of 1957, John Peter pointed to a useful distinction. "Fables," he said, "are those narratives which leave the impression that their purpose was anterior, some initial thesis or contention which they are apparently concerned to embody and express in concrete terms." Fiction is quite different. "Here the author's aim ... is evidently to present a more or less faithful reflection of the complexities, and often of the irrelevancies, of life as it is actually experienced." According to this definition *The Lord of the Flies* is a fable, as is also *Paradise Lost* and *The Cocktail Party*, while Lawrence's *The Rainbow* and Wordsworth's *Prelude* are clearly fiction.

The distinction is worth making, so long as it is remembered that the fabulist may be interested in the specific vehicle which carries his abstraction, and that the writer of fiction does not normally confront experience like a tape recorder, without deciding beforehand what data he intends to recognize. But it cannot be denied that Golding is a fabulist in a special sense, though certainly not as La Fontaine was a fabulist. It is obvious that Golding selects that fragment of human experience which will express his moral themes, and he does so as Jesus used parables, or the village schoolmaster an illustrative anecdote— because he has designs on us. Because his novels have something of the quality of a riddle to be solved, or a code to be broken, they have been popular with teachers of English courses who like ambiguity, irony, and levels of meaning.

Certainly Golding is a fabulist, if some reservations are made. If Coleridge were to review one of Golding's novels, he would no doubt have called him an allegorist, rather than a fabulist, on the grounds that fables should use conventional symbols which have been long established: "It may indeed be justly said, that in a fable no allegoric agent or image should be used which has not had some paramount quality universally attributed to it beforehand, while in an allegory the resemblance may have been presented for the first time by the writer. This is the true cause why animals, the heathen gods, and trees, the properties of which are recalled by their very names, are almost the only proper *dramatis personae* of a fable." Golding, then, is an inventive fabulist, like Faulkner and Camus, rather than a traditional fabulist like Aesop or George Orwell.

On other grounds it is necessary to say that *fables* is an inadequate term for the kind of writing produced by Golding. Fables contain folk wisdom, and both situation and character are reduced to a kind of abstract representativeness in order to insure a universal impact. There is always the peril of losing the connection between the action and the idea it illumines. The specialty of fables is the cunning of Ulysses, rather than the wisdom of Plato: they would have been written by Benjamin Franklin, if he had in addition to his other gifts a sense of narrative. They give us helpful advice on the art of living, and seem all to have been written by a foxy Grandpa. In the characteristic fable of the hare and the tortoise, the limitation of the genre is obvious: the subtlety of development is sacrificed in order to make the simplest point, that perseverance pays. But Golding has in mind another kind of truth.

Finally, fables have a contrived, artificial air which offends the sensibilities of both reader and writer. In an interview for *Books and Art* in March, 1958, he said that the problem facing modern humanity was that of learning to live fearlessly with the natural chaos of existence, without trying to impose on experience an artificial pattern. The previous year he wrote in *The London Magazine* (May, 1957) that he had a serious, Aeschylean preoccupation with the human tragedy:

> I can't help feeling that critics of this Aeschylean outlook are those who think they have an easy answer to all the problems simply because they have never looked further than the rash appearing on the skin.

Any modern writer would wince if a label were applied to him which meant that he had reduced the complexity of his subject to the morality of a Sunday School class on a thin day.

Golding would prefer to be thought of as a myth-maker. The difference between fable and myth is that the latter is not a clever story, like the fox and the grapes, but a primordial truth that seems to arise from the depths of human experience with a

8

power of explaining everything before and after. The game he would bag is not the gnomic truth that could be framed and hung on the wall, but the mythic truth that lies at the edge of human consciousness and yet serves as a key to the vast riddle. "In all my books," he said, "I have suggested a shape in the universe that may account for things." The key to his intention, and to his ultimate sobriety as an artist, is that he looks for a story which grips our interest and is at the same time a total explanation, like Plato's myth of the cave or his myth of the charioteer. "What I would regard as a tremendous compliment to myself," he told an interviewer on a BBC program, "would be if someone would substitute the word 'myth' for 'fable' . . . . I do feel fable as being an invented thing on the surface, whereas myth is something which comes from the roots of things in the ancient sense of being the key to existence, the whole meaning of life, and experience as a whole."

The problem of finding the exact word for his kind of novel is difficult. *Fable* is slightly wrong, and *myth* will not quite do. He has proposed as an appropriate tag "myths of total explanation," but surely the phrase is too big to use except at a testimonial dinner. Samuel Hynes proposed the word "tropological," which suggests the shape of the universe; or, if that seems too "rarefied," he offered "moral models." None of these have the quality of comprehension and inevitability that he would like, and so perhaps we shall have to settle for a looser term, allegory, perhaps, or the novel *à thèse*. In any case, what is necessary at the beginning of our study is to observe Golding's general character as a storyteller who proposes to convey the gnomic wisdom that settles the human predicament. He asks to be judged not simply as an entertainer, but as one who entertains in order to present an icon of the real word; and so he challenges comparison with such paradigmatic storytellers as Camus and Kafka.

We turn then to an examination of the Golding *oeuvre*. What we have said of his intention has restricted the scope of our criticism. We may find that the pattern he proposes is too oppressive, or too tiny to subsume the proliferation of experience, but we surely cannot find that the effort is timid or trivial. Golding's largesse of spirit, which leads him to turn from the intrigues of the bedroom or the marketplace to the cosmic drama has given grounds for the belief that he is one of the most exciting of living novelists.

The Power of Beelzebub

The book which succeeded Salinger's *Catcher in the Rye* as the book most often discussed in Student Unions, English literature classrooms, and literary seminars, was *The Lord of the Flies*. Why the book should have sold so modestly when it appeared in 1955, and why it became a *succès d'estime* a decade later, is a problem in literary double-take which I leave to literary historians and owners of bookshops. Whatever the answer, *Lord of the Flies* fascinated the critical intelligence of the middle sixties.

Its theme was the death of innocence. Possibly the secret of the book's appeal was the obscure congruence between its thesis and the social history of our land. It has often been observed that we Americans moved through a similar crisis in our national history, having passed through the bland insouciance of our pioneer days to the reluctant maturity that we now enjoy as a world power. Our national novels have often portrayed this ripening of the ingenue: *Huckleberry Finn, The Great Gatsby, Catcher in the Rye*. In each case the hero loses his Adamic innocence and takes an awkward role in the world of grown-ups. The *Spannung* between the fragile structures of society and the primordial vitalities which explode beneath them is part of the American saga, exemplified in Western stories as well as in our political life; and it is the theme also of *Lord of the Flies*.

Golding's novel is about a company of English schoolboys, refugees from an atomic war, who have been deposited for safe-keeping on an uninhabited island of the South Seas. Attempting to carry on in the traditions of home before the holocaust, they organize into a makeshift community in order to

11

find food and shelter and to tend the signal fire which will lead to their rescue. But dissension springs up among the boys. Worse still, an unspeakable threat appears on the mountain. By degrees the boys degenerate from the carefree lads of the opening chapter, frolicking like choirboys on a picnic, to the savage killers of the final chapter, who stalk their prey like animals.

Ralph is the boys' choice as leader. He is a tall, good-looking twelve-year-old who struggles to keep a minimal order, but who cannot understand or deal with the wild, subterranean forces that threaten his command. He is helped by Piggy, a fat asthmatic proto-intellectual who uses his thick glasses to start the signal fire; and by Simon, a frail, Christlike figure who despite his shyness is the only boy brave enough to climb the mountain and confront the nameless terror thought to be there.

Leading the disruptive forces is Jack Merridew, a coarse redhead whose chagrin at not being chosen leader causes him to neglect the signal fire and to turn his food hunters into a terroristic band. As the novel opens he approaches with some marching choirboys from "the darkness of the forest." At first Jack cannot see Ralph, whose back is to the sun. Significantly his first command to the choirboys is that they remove their robes, which are marked with the sign of the cross. His confederate is Roger, a sadist, who later becomes the murderer of Piggy.

The novel clearly is about the fortunes of a few individuals who are at the same time representative people: singular little boys, who are also exemplars of the conservatives, the intellectuals, the criminals. Golding is clearly concerned with a universal theme, but his setting—an island like Tahiti—is strikingly vivid and comes alive for us like a successful Kodachrome: and his action—the refuge from an atomic blast—has also a singular quality, never having happened elsewhere. Always there is a contrapuntal motion between the odd and the familiar. As in *King Lear,* the underlying theme is the descent into animality. Chapter One, "The Sound of the Shell," introduces the conch that the boys use to call assemblies and to recognize speakers in

12

the forum, thus serving in the novelist's shorthand for decorum, sanity, and free speech in a free society; the last chapter is "The Cry of Hunters," and between these chapters the democratic society has become a wolf pack. The agent for this deterioration is "the Thing," a nameless Beast or malignancy that seems to live on the mountain and turns what might have been a paradise à la Gaugin into an island hell. He is Beelzebub, whom the Pharisees called "prince of the devils," by etymology "Lord of the Flies," the Miltonic deity who presides over offal and carrion.

Golding has taken a steady look at the mystery of evil: the ancestral bias toward death and destruction that lurks just below the surface of polite behavior, biding its time, until a flaw appears in the conventions of society and the obscene deity appears. His archetypal topic—the loss of innocence—has been documented as well by Henry James, Conrad, Faulkner, Malraux, Camus, Graham Greene, and is certainly part of the distinctive anxiety of our time. The special kind of evil—the terrifying loss of humanity suffered by survivors of an atomic blast—is also the theme of Aldous Huxley's *Ape and Essences* (1948) and Walter M. Miller's *A Canticle for Leibowitz* (1959).

But *Lord of the Flies* is descended directly from the archetype of all such adventures, Daniel De Foe's *Robinson Crusoe* (1719). De Foe drew the rough outline that many lesser hands have filled in: there is a disaster that spares a few survivors, there is a lucky landing on an island that turns out to be a place of safety but also a place of mysterious danger, there is a struggle before the eventual rescue. Crusoe is the quintessential Englishman, who believes in God but who does not waste time brooding about Beelzebub and Gabriel. He busies himself instead by turning his primitive acre into a copy of a Sussex farm. Not only is his English common sense on his side, but God is there too. More ready than Golding to ascend a pulpit, De Foe tells the story, as he explains in his preface, "to justify the Wisdom of Providence in all the Variety of our Circumstance."

More immediately, *Lord of the Flies* is descended from an adventure story read by English boys and girls for a century, R. M. Ballantyne's *The Coral Island* (1857). Ballantyne thinks his boys are equal to the situation, whether God is helping or not. In his book Jack, age eighteen, is the natural leader who commands with a common sense which validates itself. Ralph, the narrator, is fifteen, but he navigates the schooner back from an exploring trip by dead reckoning; Peterkin is the useful pig-killer. There is danger from visiting savages and from pirates, but the boys are equal to the threat. Written during the full exuberance of Victorian imperialism, the book is a classical "Robinsonade," and Ballantyne never doubts that a public school discipline could subdue a native disturbance, just as easily as Robinson Crusoe built his rustic paradise and rescued Friday. What possible threat could survive the combined attack of Anglo-Saxon ingenuity, a tradition of justice impartially administered, a stiff upper lip, and possibly also a Providence anxious that goodness should win?

Golding replies, "Evil." *Lord of the Flies* is related to *The Coral Island* as Orwell's *Nineteen Eighty-Four* is related to *Rebecca of Sunnybrook Farm*. "Would you like to see what schoolboys are really like?" Golding seems to ask, and we recall that he was for many years a schoolmaster. Vaughan's children come wreathed in light, and Wordsworth's children trail clouds of glory, but Golding's children smell of sulphur and sweaty sneakers and beckon towards Gehenna. They are very like the children in Richard Hughes' novel, *A High Wind in Jamaica* (1929), who are such little fiends that they shock even the pirates! But Golding does not intend us to say, "Children are like that until they grow up." The boys are rescued by adults, but they are in this plight because of a grown-ups' war, and the destroyer which rescues them is itself on a manhunt not unlike that organized by Jack.

The rich concretion of event and character in the novel offers the same possibilities of interpretation that life itself affords. It is inviting, for example, to think of the book as a political allegory. The degeneration of the boys is very like the degener-

14

ation of Germany under Adolf Hitler. Trace the gradual demonization of the Third Reich, from the *Urgemütlichkeit* of Bavaria, the waltz, the October fest, the cuckoo clock, to the ovens at Dachau and you will have charted the demonization of Golding's novel. When Jack orders the innocent Wilfred beaten, he seems the quintessential Gestapo agent, beating his pistol butt against the civilized doors of the West.

Or one might read the novel as an attack upon the imperialist ideal. Anticipated by De Foe and luminous in Ballantyne, there was a nineteenth-century conviction that the white man's burden would be easily borne, that the savage corners of the earth would succumb to the attraction of the cult of the gentleman, and that in time the jungles of the world could be ridden in as safely as Regent's Park. But the civilizing dream proved only that. Wild demonries struggled to the surface and erupted as Communism, or Fascism, or a thankless Nationalism that wanted nothing of England. If the structure of order is not ruthlessly preserved, as Shakespeare's Ulysses told his fellow Greeks,

> The rude son should strike his father dead,
> And strength should be lord of imbecility.

Against the resulting convulsive disorder the restraint of English culture is helpless. To expect more of it is to make the mistake of the naval officer who rescues Golding's boys and says, "I should have thought that a pack of English boys . . . would have put up a better show."

Another style of interpretation makes use of the conceptual formulae of the social psychologists. It is tempting to see Freudian depths in several of the incidents, even though Golding has disowned this intention. Writing in the *Spectator* on September 7, 1962, he said that he was surprised when students in creative writing courses in American colleges seemed preoccupied with sex symbolism. He also told a lecture audience that he had read no Freud. But Viennese psychology hangs in the air, and *Lord of the Flies* makes use of several Freudian insights. The episode of the killing of the sow, for instance, is borrowed from Ballantyne, except that Golding describes the kill in terms of sexual fulfillment. And "the Thing" is a Freudian taboo, the forbidden object for which there exists a strong inclination in the unconscious.

The novel also illustrates the theory of play in Freud, namely, that children act out situations which impress them, and so acquire mastery over them. Their games are examples of "the omnipotence of thought," which is best exemplified in art. The novel also bears out the analysis of play in Johan Huizinga's *Homo Ludens* (1955). Jack and his hunters ritualize the hunting of the pig. According to Huizinga, early play is a deliberate stepping out of life, and is always known to be pretending. Gradually play becomes ritual, and the action which the play represents becomes more and more blurred. Momentary remembrance of the original occasion causes some restraint of the play, and there are times when the mimetic character of the play comes to the fore. Thus when an older boy in Golding's novel throws a stone at a younger boy, "there was a space around Henry, perhaps six yards in diameter, into which he dare not throw. Here invisible yet strong, was the taboo of the old life. Round the squatting child was the protection of parents and school and police men and the law." Because game and reality are in the early stages kept distinct, Jack hesitates to plunge his knife into the first pig, just as the boys hesitated in *The Coral Island*.

But the line between play and life becomes faint. The pig hunt had begun as a search for food. Jack and his killers then re-enact the hunting, assigning to one boy the role of the pig. They take up the ritual shout, "Kill the pig. Cut her throat. Bash her in." The chant, like Hitler's brief slogans (or like a college cheer), has the effect of a charm. At the edge of rational discourse, it is more like a scream than a statement, and it moves towards hysteria. "Kill him! kill him!" the boys shout, as once the mob shouted at Golgotha. According to the logic of demagoguery, the spasmodic cries set up a participation mystique, reinforced by the anguish of the dance. The hypnotic incantation, the pulsating dance rhythms, the appeal to sub-

16

rational violence works with explosive power, and even the horrified Ralph, watching from the sidelines, finds himself stirred. Jack's assassins move imperceptibly from playing children to ritual murderers, and the slaying of Piggy and Simon seems at the end like a fitting prolongation. Whereas at the beginning stage the play imitates life, at the end Jack's convulsive life imitates the game.

A primary Freudian problem lies deeply buried in *Lord of the Flies*. The question has to do with the locus of the disruptive, evil forces that terrify the boys. Are they objective, real in the sense that they exist whether feared by the boys or not? Or are they projections of adolescent fright, bogey men who people the hovering mountain because the boys put them there? Freud's answer had the dogmatic tone that he always assumed when he was not really sure. "It would be different," he wrote in *Totem and Taboo*, "if demons really existed; but we know that, like gods, they are really only the products of the psychic powers of men."

If the demons were real the problem would indeed be different; but this is precisely what we do not know. Ralph sees the centrality of the problem, and violates the taboo to ask his intellectual friend Piggy about it: "The trouble is: are there ghosts, Piggy? Or beasts?" Piggy, wise for his years, has solved the question along Freudian lines; he has no room in his rational, ordered universe for the absurd. An irrational element, like the notion of a preternatural power, scrambles all the logical equations on which the humanist universe is built. " 'Cos things wouldn't make sense," he explains. "Houses, an'—TV— they wouldn't work." This boyish philosopher has gone too far, since it is quite possible to believe both in an orderly universe of law and in the possibility of supernatural revelation; but he is quite right that any notion of the preternatural threatens the inevitable operation of natural laws.

What his rationalist faith does not take into account, and what Ralph's common sense cannot perceive, is that there might be supernatural influences both in the orderly processes of nature and in the miraculous interruptions of those processes, and what both Ralph and Piggy have failed to take into account is the demonic depth which is only partly concealed by nature's repetitions and by the conventions of men. They both underestimate the chthonic power of evil and exaggerate the power of plain truth. When Hitler rose to power the German universities thought that they could overthrow him with the massed power and dignity of thought; when Jack threatened the island with chaos, Piggy thought, "I'm going to him with this conch in my hands . . . . What's right's right." He thinks of the world as a quiet classroom where what is right wins, and so he rashly concludes, "I know there isn't no beast . . . but I know there is no fear, either . . . unless we get frightened of people."

Simon alone faces the terror. In Chapter 5, after the assembly called by Ralph has voted for the belief in ghosts, Simon grants the presence of terror, but thinks that "maybe it's only us." In order to find out the truth, he slips off by himself to climb the magic mountain (for all the world like Moses at Sinai) in order to bring back the news of whatever truth he would find. He comes down from the mountain with the truth about the fallen parachutist; but instead of being hailed as a savior who has dispelled the darkness, he is received exactly as is the man in Plato's allegory of the cave who returns from the daylight to tell the others they are looking at shadows; he is stoned to death.

Ironically, it is the degenerate Jack who knows that the beast exists outside himself. At first his plan is to hunt the thing. When this proves futile ("we wrestle not against flesh and blood," said St. Paul, "but against . . . the rulers of darkness"), he thinks he can drive it out of his thoughts: "We're going to forget the beast," he tells his followers, and "they agree passionately out of the depth of their tormented lives." When the Thing cannot be so simply exorcised, he turns to techniques of propitiation, leaving part of their kill behind for it, and dancing and chanting wildly to placate it. Jack and Roger, simply by knowing themselves, are aware of a depth of evil that is hidden from Ralph and Piggy, with their sentimental confidence in civilized structures. "The theme," said Golding in reply to a recent questionnaire, "is an attempt to trace the defects of society back to the defects of human nature. The moral is that the shape of a society must depend on the ethical nature of the individual and not on any political system however apparently logical or respectable."

It is part of Golding's achievement that like all the great storytellers he enchants his listeners, and they feel themselves involved in what happens to these boys at this place at this time. It is only when he has finished that the reader wonders about the appropriate generalization which is supported by the exemplum he has just read. Perhaps only the professional critic feels called upon not only to respond to the book with pleasure or pain or boredom, but also to explain what the book has said and whether he can approve or not.

When such an effort is made, the reader understands that Golding has made an assertion about evil, which he takes to be part of the data of experience. This evil is not an external power or presence (there are no ghosts), nor is it a defect of political or social structures (no matter what society man constructs, the evil will show itself). But the evil is real, and may be called Beelzebub, Lord of the Flies.

How then shall Beelzebub be chained? Certainly not by social conventions such as culture, education, or systems of law, since the evil can use even these for its obscure purpose. Not by common sense, either, as Ralph, Piggy, and Simon discover; the silken thread of reason cannot bind the raging beast. Nor by ritual propitiation, as Jack and Roger believe, since these gestures serve only to exacerbate the problem, whetting the appetite for blood and power. Where then can help be found? What passing cruiser can rescue not only the boys from their evil, but the adults as well?

Golding does not say. Content to light a signal fire, he warns of disruptive forces that defy the normal disciplinary instruments. He sees rightly with Hobbes that evil is within man, and the rescue by the government cruiser is perhaps his concession to Hobbes' belief that the strong ruler can set matters right. But he does not sufficiently realize that the evil is outside man as well, so that man not only projects evil, but is also sometimes seized by it, as the Nazis undoubtedly were seized by demonic forces in our time. The evil in the world has its intricate power because it takes so many forms, sometimes being projected by man in sheer malice, and sometimes seizing men who are helpless before it, and sometimes being imagined by men when there is nothing to fear. Against this supernatural brilliance the cunning of man is not enough.

The missing piece from Golding's puzzle, the denouement which would properly have resolved his plot, is St. Paul's insight that supernatural aid is necessary to do battle with supernatural powers. Had the problem been correctly identified, he would have been led inevitably to the *solutio Christi,* which Milton recognized as the massive answer to Beelzebub:

> Leader of these Armies bright
> Which but the Omnipotent none could have foyld.

Before and After History

The device of studying the human condition by isolating a group of boys on an uninhabited island was a brilliant invention, providing exotic detail, vivid situations, and numerous parallels to the situations of adults in their everyday world. In his next novel Golding again chose an unusual situation, this time throwing unexpected light on the human adventure by imagining what the world was like at the very moment when human beings entered history by crushing their immediate predecessors, the Neanderthals. With admirable audacity he set his characters moving and speaking *am Ersten Tag,* almost before there were words, just after the morning stars sang together.

As *Lord of the Flies* was an occasional work, brought into being to refute Ballantyne's *The Coral Island,* so *The Inheritors* was written to give the lie to H. G. Wells. The motto of the book is a quotation from *The Outline of History*:

> We know very little of the appearance of the Neanderthal man, but this . . . seems to suggest an extreme hairiness, an ugliness, or a repulsive strangeness in his appearance over and above his low forehead, his beetle brows, his ape neck, and his inferior stature.

Wells then goes on to quote with approval a remark made by Henry Johnston in *Views and Reviews:*

> The dim racial remembrance of such gorilla-like monsters, with cunning brains, shambling gait, hairy bodies, strong teeth, and possibly cannibalistic tendencies, may be the germ of the ogre in folklore.

In a later autobiographical essay, Golding tells why he disliked H. G. Wells: "Wells's *Outline* played a large part in my life because my father was a rationalist, and the *Outline* was

21

something he took neat. It is the rationalist gospel *in excelsis.* . . . By and by it seemed to me not to be large enough . . . too neat and too slick. And when I re-read it as an adult I came across his picture of Neanderthal man, our immediate predecessors, as being these gross brutal creatures who were possibly the basis of the mythological bad men . . . I thought to myself that this is just absurd."

Wells was an ardent spokesman for the doctrine of progress, according to which history is the record of man's slow painful ascent from animality to a full human dignity, marked by rational control. His short story "The Grisly Folk" is also about the encounter between the Neanderthals and *homo sapiens,* but unlike Golding, his sympathies are with the first man, who is not only later in time but higher on the evolutionary ladder, bearing in his seed the promise of civilization. Golding's more orthodox doctrine of the Fall led him to the opposite point of view: in his imagination Neanderthal man was an innocent prelapsarian who lived in a state of gentle innocence until corrupted and destroyed by the more wicked and more powerful human beings. The simple plot of *The Inheritors* is that "the People," as he calls his Neanderthals, move to a new feeding-ground in the spring of the year and encounter "the new people," humans, who by virtue of greater cunning destroy the Neanderthal colony.

The technical problems involved in writing a novel about a preconceptual culture are formidable, and the fact that Golding even tried speaks much for his creative vitality. How can one describe the faint stirrings of mind in a people who cannot yet be said to think, and who know only a few sounds that could be called words? Golding's people think—if what goes on in their ape-like skulls can be called thought—by means of a sequence of pictures and by means of a conditioned memory:

"I have a picture—"

Then the people laughed too because this was Lok's picture, almost the only one he had, and they knew it as well as he did. "—a picture of finding the little Oa."

22

If no one can be sure that this is how Neanderthals thought, neither can anyone deny that this might be a correct account. It is certainly possible that in the absence of any conventional abstractions and in the absence of an accepted grammar their communications were largely pictorial. In any event, Golding succeeds remarkably in conveying a primitive reflection which is so feeble and intermittent that it can hardly be distinguished from bare existence, like a stone in a brook or a cat by the fire, and yet does not suggest moronic stupidity. There is a wisdom here, though it has not yet found articulation:

> They flexed their toes and stretched their arms, even leaning away from the fire. One of the deep silences fell on them, that seemed so much more natural than speech, a timeless silence in which there were at first many minds in the overhang; and then perhaps no mind at all.

But though Lok cannot converse like Coleridge at Highgate, his people do have a style of life, and even a code of ethics that is simple but authoritative. They are vegetarians out of reverence for life. On the rare occasions when they do eat meat, it is only when they come across an animal that has already been killed. So great is their natural dignity that they will not take the life of any living thing, which they believe came from the great belly of Oa and so had a supernatural commission to live. Oa is their great primal deity, like Gea, the Earth Mother, who gives life and takes life. When Mal dies after his soaking in the cold river he is buried with solemn dignity and is received by Oa's great womb.

A simple hylozoism gives to their days an unfailing excitement: logs, fires, stones have personalities of their own and are called good or bad according to their willingness to serve the people. The people have a quietly happy family life, despite their many physical discomforts; each member of the family has an assigned role, and there is a delicately adjusted tradition of rights and duties. Though it runs to slapstick, they have a sense of humor; when the bridge is missing, Lok has to deny that he removed it "to make the people laugh." They make love tenderly without shame or guilt, with the same unstudied directness that they breathe and eat. They are without sin, like animals and flowers, and only their difficulty in finding food and keeping warm keeps their state from seeming paradisaical.

But when the first whiff of the new people makes their nostrils quiver, the quality of terror enters their history for the first time. The new people, the inheritors, walk stiffly upright, balancing their white heads and peering out over arched noses and bony cheeks. The newcomers wear fur clothes against the chill, decorate themselves with jewelry, move over water in dugout canoes, and strike from a distance with bows and arrows. Unlike the Neanderthals, they kill. Whereas Wells has his Neanderthals steal a human baby, Golding has his human beings steal the Neanderthal baby, Liku. *Homo sapiens* have the gift of reason and language, but use it foolishly. They quarrel and fight, and their love-making is more like anger. They are cruel and timid and they shake with guilt and anxiety.

Watching the human beings from a safe hiding place, Lok and Fa begin to lose their virginal innocence and at last become almost as wicked as men. They learn to associate sex with cruelty. They sample the sickness and the excitement of drunkenness. They begin to compare one picture with another, and so achieve a kind of rudimentary thought:

> Lok discovered "Like." He had used likeness all his life without being aware of it. Fungi on trees were ears, the word was the same but acquired a distinction that could never apply to the sensitive things on the side of the head. Now, like a convulsion of the understanding Lok found himself using likeness as a tool as surely as ever he had used a stone to hack at sticks or meat. . . ."The people are like a famished wolf in the hollow of a tree."

Somewhere ahead, down the long corridor of history, lies the Homeric simile, the Shakespearian metaphor, and Butler's doctrine of analogy.

What can one say about *The Inheritors?* Frank Kermode thinks highly of it. *"The Inheritors,"* he said, "is Mr. Golding's most perfect book, ambitious in design and of terrific imaginative force. Though, since it is concerned only with the

24

Fall and not with The Last Things, it offers a less complete account of the Golding world than *Pincher Martin*." I cannot agree. In some fanciful novels which empirical Englishmen produce (Tolkien's *Lord of the Rings,* Williams' *War in Heaven*, Lewis's *Perelandra*) the reader suspends his disbelief and enters a magic world that has its own credibility. But the world of *The Inheritors* seems strange to the very end. The difficulty is that we can never quite believe in "the people." We do not make the cry of excited assent, "Surely this is how it was!" but rather make the grudging admission that it may have been so. On the other hand, Neanderthals may have been as unattractive as Wells thought. Since we have no way of settling the matter, we lose interest in the problem.

In other words, we admire *The Inheritors* as a *tour de force,* rather than as a clue to the human character. Tuami and his fellow human beings are unmistakably creatures of Golding's teeming fancy, made up out of his head with very little to go on; but they are for that reason not much help in deciding whether human nature is steadily improving or getting worse or staying the same. We have something at stake in this question, in fact a great deal; but we have no confidence in Golding's answer. It is perhaps this fatal defect that arms the reader with an unremitting detachment, so that his eye moves over many long passages without his mind knowing what is happening, but also without a sense of deprivation.

Golding's third novel continued his experiment of learning about the human normality by looking at a kind of existence deliberately chosen because it lies beyond the bright circle of ordinary life. *Lord of the Flies* looked like an adventure story for and about boys, but it turned out to be concerned with problems of human evil that no boy ever worried about; *The Inheritors* was about the death of the Neanderthals, but it proved really to be a homily on human evil; *Pincher Martin* is about the adventures of a man after he has died. It is possible to demonstrate that each of these bold efforts failed in some measure, but it is not possible to deny the audacity of the imagination that dared such flights. The literary West knew that it was in the presence of a major creative talent.

Pincher Martin has the simple, uncluttered narrative line that Golding always adopts, and that serves so well as a framework for subtleties of analysis that might otherwise prove intolerable. A wartime naval officer is on a destroyer that is torpedoed in mid-Atlantic. Though his chances for survival seem nil, he is miraculously cast up on a barren rock called "Rockall"; but he is by no means safe, because he is threatened by the sea, by the burning sun, by the cold of the nights, by the scarcity of food and drink, and by the disintegration of his mental processes.

Having an indomitable will to survive (the subject fascinates Golding and provides the matter for his first three novels), he uses all his ingenuity to cling to a minimal existence despite impossible circumstances. He eats algae, sea anemones, seaweed, and shellfish. He drinks from pools of rainwater. He finds shelter in a crevice in the rock. When constipation sets in, he performs successfully a homemade enema. What he cannot prevent is the gradual debilitation of his body and the disorder of his mind, pulling him farther away from reality. Just before the end his mind snaps, unable to preserve the usual logical sequences in such a hopeless setting.

The last chapter makes use of what has been now become a Golding trademark: an abrupt change in the point of view from which the central action of the novel is seen from a fresh perspective. In *Lord of the Flies*, the viewpoint at the end is that of the adult naval officer who rescues the boys; in *The Inheritors* the viewpoint shifts from the Neanderthals to the first human beings; and in *Pincher Martin* the scene shifts to the Outer Hebrides, where an official finds a body drifting in the sea and which he identifies as that of naval officer Christopher Martin. A Mr. Campbell wonders whether the officer suffered much before he died. Mr. Davidson reassures him: "You saw the body. He didn't even have time to kick off his seaboots."

This is a strange bit of information that has puzzled readers. Early in the first chapter we were told that the stricken officer had with some difficulty kicked off his seaboots in order to stay afloat. How can one explain their presence on his feet when the body was found? It is possible, of course, that Golding nodded; he had forgotten the item of the footgear by the time he wrote the last chapter. But too much is made of the detail, both at the beginning and at the end, and Golding is a careful workman. The more likely explanation is that Golding put in the ambiguity purposely, and the title he chose for the American edition makes the point clear: *The Two Deaths of Christopher Martin.* The hero dies instantly, perhaps at the moment when the destroyer explodes, and the novel is about a dead man; but in some unsolved way he dies a second death after six days of some kind of life on Rockall. Oblivion does not follow the heart's last flutter. There is existence, though the mind hovers in a dreamlike state and matter has a surrealistic, nightmarish quality. After Pincher's first death a lobster sits patiently on his trousers, and this lobster is red; the rock is very like a decaying tooth, and may in fact be a decaying tooth; guano now is insoluble; lightning rips the great sky, but it is colored black. The parts of the familiar world are here—except for human fellowship—but all the parts are distorted, like fragments of a madman's dream.

Pincher Martin is dead, and the novel is about a corpse. But what kind of corpse is as busy as this one, eating, hunting, dreaming, cursing? In the summer of 1957, writing in the *Kenyon Review*, Wayland Young suggested that the story was about Pincher's Purgatory, and an authoritative letter in the *Times Literary Supplement* on August 28, 1959, stated flatly that Pincher had died at the beginning of the novel, and that the rest of the story dealt with Purgatory. It is possible that Golding has this state in mind, and if so it would fit his pattern of turning theological abstractions into concrete detail. But if this is what he meant he certainly had a faulty notion of Purgatory. According to the traditional teaching, Purgatory is a state of suffering after death (which fits the case of Pincher Martin), but it is only for those Christians who die in venial sin, or who die

27

before they can complete their temporal punishment for mortal sin, and so must have a period of time to complete their preparation for heaven, using also the suffrages of living friends. But when the destroyer sinks, Pincher Martin dies unrepentant in mortal sin. He has chosen evil, the matter is weighty (nothing less than murder), and he has made no single act of contrition. He was not qualified for Purgatory.

The simpler explanation is that the novel is about hell, as Charles Williams' *Terror of Sight* is about the hell at the bottom of the sea, where the damned creep about between and under stones. In fact, Golding said that "Pincher is simply in hell. The whole of *Pincher Martin* is Pincher's *post mortem* experience of himself." The usual view of hell has traditional trappings, many of them derived from Dante and the pop art of the middle ages: there is a handsome devil in evening dress but with a tail and cloven hoofs, there is an everlasting fire, there are screams. "But your purgatory, or your heaven," said Golding, "won't have to have the Christian attributes." What we have before us is a modern sermon on hellfire and brimstone, though it seems at first a place more friendly and manageable than the traditional hell. The exquisite horror of this special hell only becomes apparent to us as we watch Pincher's deliberate reduction of all objective reality to solipsism. He is St. Augustine's *amor sui* seen with our eyes and felt along the nerves.

Golding has never been averse to adding critical comment to his own artistic creations, and during a dramatization of the novel on a B.B.C. program, he provided this comment:

"Christopher Hadley Martin had no belief in anything but the importance of his own life; no love, no God. Because he was created in the image of God he had a freedom of choice which he used to centre the world on himself. He did not believe in purgatory and therefore when he died it was not presented to him in overtly theological terms. The greed for life which had been the mainspring of his nature, forced him to refuse the selfless act of dying. He continued to exist separately in a world composed of his own murderous nature. His

28

drowned body lies rolling in the Atlantic but the ravenous ego invents a rock for him to endure on. It is the memory of an aching tooth. Ostensibly and rationally he is a survivor from a torpedoed destroyer: but deep down he knows the truth. He is not fighting for bodily survival but for his continuing identity in [the] face of what will smash it and sweep it away—the black lightning, the compassion of God. For Christopher, the God-bearer, has become Pincher Martin, who is little but greed. Just to be Pincher is Purgatory; to be Pincher for eternity is hell."

While all living things have an impulse to survive, Pincher Martin's greed for life is an expression of his obsessive self-centeredness. Having rejected God as well as the created universe of people and things, he has at last only the company of himself. But the self that converses with him in memory is not good company: he meets a thief, an adulterer, a rapist, and a potential murderer. A fellow amateur actor sums up his essential character: "This painted bastard here takes anything he can lay his hands on. Not food, Chris, that's far too simple. He takes the best part, the best seat, the most money, the best notice, the best woman. He was born with his mouth and his fly open and both hands out to grab." When Golding was asked about his non-hero he replied that Pincher was "a fallen man . . . very much fallen—he's fallen more than most."

At the end of the novel, when Pincher has a final encounter with God, who is now dressed as a sailor, God asks him what he believes in. "The thread of my life," replies Pincher. "I have created you and I can create my own heaven."

"You *have* created it," says God.

The catch is that Pincher's heaven is really hell. "Hell is one's self," as one of Eliot's characters says; but one may also say "Hell is the others," as a character in Sartre's *No Exit* says. Both are true, since the resources neither of selfhood nor of social intercourse are sufficient to support the curiosity of eternity. Pincher has pursued the logic of a human universe to its absurd end, and has developed his selfhood to the point where it beckons toward the ultimate idiocy, where the outside world

29

disappears and there is nothing left but the unspeakable tedium of death. Fire is bad enough, and Dante's ice will also suffice; but neither is so terrible as Pincher's world after God's rock and sea and sun disappear, leaving in their place the quintessential nothingness. The final horror of hell is that it is chosen, and that it leads at last to an undifferentiated emptiness in which the least recognizable thing, even pain, would be welcomed as an act of His terrible mercy.

The Death of Innocence

Free Fall (1959) was the first of Golding's novels to use a modern setting and contemporary, naturalistic episodes. What happens to Sammy Mountjoy could happen to anyone. The narrator tells the story of his life, selecting certain episodes without regard for chronological order but because they seem crucial in his career. A bare summary of his autobiography is that he was born in a slum somewhere in Kent, the son of an unknown father and a prostitute. Urged on by a mischievous companion, he desecrates a church, is caught, and is given a cuff on the ear that causes an infection. He is adopted by a vicar who seems to have homosexual tendencies as well as delusions of persecution. He seduces a chapel girl named Beatrice, tires of her, leaves her, and finds out later that she has lost her mind. He marries a girl named Taffy, and they have one child. He tries Communism for a while, learns how to be a commercial artist and gets a commission in the armed forces as combat artist. He is captured by the Germans and thrown into solitary confinement when he will not (or cannot) inform on his comrades who are planning an escape.

Sammy's purpose in picking through the ragbag of his experience is to find out whether or not there is any pattern in his history. Like all artists and intellectuals, he has a rage for order: he rebels against the improvised drift of line, color, and event, and wonders if the discrete incidents of his life could be fitted together like the pieces of a jigsaw puzzle. His quest invites comparison with Marcel Proust, who set out to look through what St. Augustine called "the palace of memory" in order to find out if the boy who once tasted the madeleine cake was the same as the man who now tasted it. Samuel Beckett developed the same theme in *Krapp's Last Tape*.

When he was interviewed on a B.B.C. program a year before the publication of the novel, Golding said that his purpose was to demonstrate that life has no pattern of its own which is not imposed upon it. In fact, the distinctive quality of life is that it is without pattern. "The difference between being alive and being an inorganic substance," he said, "is just this proliferation of experience, this absence of pattern." Speaking of *Free Fall*, which he had just finished writing, he said, "This time I want to show the patternless of life before we impose our patterns on it."

One of the patterns that is used to order experience is religion. There are two religious figures in the novel, both of them unattractive. Father Watts-Watt is a pitiful priest who means well but is overcome by dark, disruptive forces that finally overthrow his sanity. The other religionist, Miss Rowena Pringle, is a teacher of religion. She is a mean, frustrated spinster, bent on finding obscenity in Sammy's drawings, and convincing even herself at the end that she has always been his friend. Her hold on the real world is almost as weak as Father Watts-Watt's.

Rationalism of the H. G. Wells variety is also a way of ordering experience. The exponent of this way of life is Mr. Nick Shales, Sammy's science teacher. Serving as a foil for Miss Pringle, he is kind, loving, generous, tolerant, and above all lucid in describing the objective world. But Sammy dimly understands that if Nick Shales is right, and if such patterns as exist in the world are put there by men, it follows that there is no real argument for morality except that it is the will of the majority. But this does not provide an adequate explanation of two qualities that Sammy thinks are important, namely, holiness and evil. Mr. Shales was a powerful influence during the school years, but later when Sammy looks him up and finds him an old man, ill and helpless, his solution to the riddle of living seems less impressive.

Sammy's obsessive idea is to fix the point at which the patterns

32

of freedom and necessity meet in his own life. He knew that there was a time of Adamic innocency, when he had the unstudied goodness of "the People" in *The Inheritors*. Golding has always been fascinated by a preconceptual kind of experience exemplified by primitive people and by infants. He finds in his own early youth the same innocence that Wordsworth studied in *The Prelude*. "I was innocent of guilt," said Sammy, "unconscious of innocence; happy, therefore, and unconscious of happiness." But he found no such innocence in his adult life. Obviously there had been a moment when he was no longer free, when innocence yielded to experience, when it was possible to accuse himself of sin. "I am looking," he wrote, "for the beginning of responsibility, the beginning of darkness, the point where I began." *Free Fall*, like Camus' novel *The Fall*, is a story about original sin, the fall that was not so much a fall as a jump, the freely chosen evil. In the language of moral theology, it is a narrative version of the transition from venial to mortal sin, and serves as a *Paradise Lost* for our time.

Sammy goes over the various episodes of his childhood—most of them unsavory—and has difficulty finding the marginal line that separates freedom from necessity. If there is any such moment, it is when he admits that he is willing to sacrifice everything for Beatrice (including his freedom), and cries out to her, "I want to be you." But the moment is not really decisive in the novel and is not presented as the crucial turning point in the story of his life. What we are presumably to understand is that there is no such pattern of freedom and necessity in Sammy's life, and that therefore the quest for the transitional point is futile. The very effort to find such a point in time is theologically naïve, and is exactly the mistake that has obscured the real profundity of the doctrine of the Fall. Original sin begins with the ascent of the semen, as St. Augustine saw, and efforts to separate in human history a time of innocency from a time of sin are as absurd as Archbishop Ussher's date for the eating of the apple in Eden (4004 B.C.). There is no temporal date for the Fall. Each human act has in it elements of innocency and elements of guilt, dialectically in tension. Golding therefore is theologically sound when he rejects the simple patterns of naive religionists like Miss Pringle, and the more attractive errors of such people as Mr. Shales, and decides instead that the complex structure of experience must be accepted, with its intermingling of sin and redemption, fall and recovery. In God's strange time I fell, I fall and I shall fall, and in my hapless soul good and evil are intermixed like Aldous Huxley's nest of intricately copulating vipers.

The theology in *Free Fall* is vague and indecisive, though in its main contours it is no doubt orthodox. But what really succeeds in the novel is the experience of the texture of living, particularly in Sammy's horrified exploration of his solitary cell. The dark terror of his solitary confinement, which has no recognizable feature and is therefore full of shapeless and nameless possibilities of evil, is perfectly transmitted to the reader, who participates in the feat with the same physical intensity that we feel when Pincher Martin crawls about his rock. If the moment when he is helpless before Beatrice marks the point of his Fall, surely the moment when he calls out from his cell "Help me! Help me!" marks the point of his redemption. "The very act of crying out," we are told, "changed the thing that cried." It is a radiant moment, comparable to the scene in Harcourt Reilly's office in *The Cocktail Party,* when Lavinia and Edward discuss their estrangement. Lavinia says, "Then what can we do, when we can go neither back nor forward? Edward! What can we do?" Whereupon Reilly says, "You have answered your own question, though you do not know the meaning of what you have said."

Sammy emerges from the cell redeemed, and the world also seems redeemed, as it did for Wesley when he emerged from the meeting in Aldersgate Street. The prison camp seemed brilliant, filled with kind and intelligent friends, and the world outside the fence seemed as though it had been spilled like jewels from a casket. Innocency is contentment which is sub-rational, like a butterfly balanced on a flower; the Fall is the moment when I make myself the absolute center, or else destroy myself altogether in the name of a symbiotic love; redemption follows

34

when I turn in desperate need to the help that others can give. Some such exegesis does justice to the exemplum of *Free Fall*.

The next novel written by Golding, *The Spire* (1964), again attempted to understand modern man by a foray into the past, this time into the fourteenth century. The subject is the building of a cathedral spire. The novel is itself a paradigm of Golding's method, since it is about a vision and its material embodiment, and throws into brilliant tension the commonplace world and the exotic dream. Golding asks the question many tourists ask when they have clambered to the top of a medieval tower: how did they manage the technical details of building so high with primitive equipment? What is the inner meaning of a cathedral spire, tall, arrogant, impractical? What happens when one deciphers a spire in terms of what the Germans call its *Kunstvollen?*

The narrative line of this novel is as usual spare. Jocelin, the Dean of Barchester Cathedral, feels himself called by God to build a spire to crown his cathedral. He is opposed by everyone—his fellow clergy, the people, the builders—all of whom point out that the foundations are too weak to support so massive a weight, and that to persist in the plan may bring the whole cathedral down in ruin. He clings to his dream, despite every kind of obstacle, and he lives just long enough to see the spire completed. The interest in the story lies in the fortunes of this fragile dream, which survives savage assaults from common sense, and finds at last its embodiment in an exultant thrust of stonework into the sky. The question Golding asks is about the validity of a seraphic logic in a world where the authoritative knowledge is thought to be scientific.

So the story is about a spire, but what Golding is really saying has to be decoded, like a message written in an unknown language on ancient stones. The story is interesting in itself, without such decoding. The town of Barchester does not exist, except in the happy land invented by Anthony Trollope, but Golding's story has its roots in what really happened. It is a matter of record that the builders of the medieval cathedrals were sometimes scandalously indifferent to their footings, according to modern standards, and many of their proudest creations float like magical ships in a sea of mud. Peterborough Cathedral was built on a peat bog; two streams flow beneath the central tower at Carlisle; Wells rises from a ring of pools as though it remains upright by a fairy's charm. It is odd that there have not been more instances of spires groaning, cracking, and sinking into the crossways with an apocalyptic roar. The Norman tower at Ely fell in 1322, giving Alan of Walsingham his chance to build the octagonal lantern; the great spire at Chichester fell in 1861, the walls bending ominously during the Christmas services, and the great mass tumbling into the nave in February.

Building spires was risky business, and Golding had facts to go on. The spire he had especially in mind was Salisbury Cathedral. He lived nearby and taught for many years in Bishop Wordsworth's School. (Incidentally, a Bishop Jocelin is buried in Salisbury.) The tallest and loveliest of English spires rises implausibly from marsh land, so that the erection, in 1330, of a four-hundred foot column of stone must have seemed to sensible people to be an act of pious madness. There is no architectural reason why Salisbury's spire should still stand, and visiting engineers cross themselves before backing hastily away; but since the first few years, when it settled twenty-three inches out of plumb, the lovely spire has held fast, as safe as a marsh hen's egg on the watery sod. One thinks of Providence, though engineers feel more confidence in the law of gravity.

The Spire is laced with odd, precise words that come directly from a medieval builder's vocabulary, but what the novel says has relevance to our own day. Readers of the book may find themselves thinking of the building of their own great-roofed church, which rose on the mud flats at the highway intersection despite the worldliness and ineptness of the building committee. They may also be reminded of Ibsen's play about another compulsive contractor, *The Master Builder*. Though both erect tall structures, both Golding's Roger Mason and Ibsen's Halvard Solness fear heights. In order to keep his builder going,

36

Dean Jocelin sacrifices the virtue of Goody Pagnall to the lust of his foreman, just as Solness sacrifices Kaia Fosli to hold his architect, Ragnar Brovik. Jocelin symbolizes the near completion of the spire by pounding a holy nail into it, while Solness hangs a wreath from the top of his tower.

The differences between *The Spire* and *The Master Builder* are also instructive. Jocelin feels that he is not his own master, but has been commissioned by an angel to build the spire; Solness had begun his career by listening to angelic voices, and had been a builder of churches, but he had turned from this occupation to that of building homes for people, and at last thought he heard demonic voices urging him to build castles in the air. Both fall tragically from their own constructions, neither having a clear notion of the relevance of the ideal world to the real world.

The Spire is also reminiscent of the late Dorothy L. Sayers' play about cathedral building, *The Zeal of Thy House*. Both use as their theme the problem of building a holy structure in medieval England with the weak instrumentality of flesh and blood. Lady Ursula de Warbois, the wealthy patron of Miss Sayers' play, has more than a coincidental similarity to Jocelin's wicked aunt. William of Sens, Miss Sayers' builder, falls from the vault into the nave and crushes his back, much as Jocelin falls and is desperately hurt. Miss Sayers' thesis—that a builder expresses his faith by what he builds, rather than by his conventional morality or his ceremonial piety—reappears in Dean Jocelin's preoccupation: he feels that his holiness must be expressed by the erection of a spire, rather than by attending cathedral services.

Salisbury spire and Ibsen and Sayers are all part of the grist for Golding's mill; but the central meaning of *The Spire* is not to be found outside the book itself. What we have before us is a remarkably clear look at the disjunction between spiritual truth and its material embodiment. The question it seeks to solve is the question that Golding has had before him from the beginning: how can an abstract truth find expression without distortion or reduction in a fictional sequence? How can the stuff of thought be presented in narrative form? He concludes that when a vision has had to become incarnate and find its place in space and time, it does so at a high price. The pure creation intended is never embodied in its purity, but must be mixed with all sorts of base alloys. And the resulting form is the work of a goodness that is not innocence, and not experience either, but something beyond both.

The dream of those anonymous men who built the medieval cathedrals far beyond their needs, and far beyond their material resources, was to translate the abstraction of faith into stone and glass and mortar. They wanted to build a structure which those who came after would think them mad to have dreamed of, and which it would not be absurd to call a house of God. "The building," explained Jocelin, "is a diagram of prayer; and our prayer will be a diagram of the highest prayer of all." So the source is an icon, a visible symbol expressing the aspiration of man for that which is beyond man. In Jocelin's vision the spire by its very absurdity would figure forth the wild sanity of prayer. A holy nail would be embedded in the spire like a saint's bone in a jewelled shrine. When the obstacles had been overcome and the spire raised, it would point like a prophet's finger to the world beyond common sense, beyond hope, beyond life itself.

Almost as plainly as the characters in the mystery plays, Jocelin stands for vision, as Roger Mason stands for common sense. The spire itself beautifully symbolizes the ambiguity of that which reaches for the stars but is at the same time dependent for its footing on the solid earth. In the builder's manuals the height of a spire must be determined not by the ambition of the builders, but by the solidity of the foundation; and in the case of Barchester the foundation was perilously loose. The lovely simplicity of the vision becomes trammelled in the complexities of mud and soil, the insolent mathematics of weight and balance, thrust and counter-thrust. Mason is the representative worldling, whose experience has been wholly in time, and whose calculations are based on the predictions of a ruthless

38

normality. He hated and feared the Dean, with his *idée fixe* of a spire that took no account of its footing, like a miracle.

Analogous to the image of the spire and its foundation is the Freudian image of man with his visible character and the hidden deeps where the true motives lurk. Jocelin is appalled that he has to construct "a building with a vast cellarage" (like the symbolic cellar in *Pincher Martin*). The model of the building described in the first chapter makes the phallic symbolism clear:

> The model was like a man lying on his back.
> The nave was his legs placed together, the transepts on either side were his arms outspread. The choir was his body, and the Lady Chapel where now the services would be held, was his head. And now also, springing, projecting, bursting, erupting from the heart of the building, there was its crown and mystery, the new spire.

Jocelin learns to distrust the simple purity of his vision as he thinks of the tangled motives of holy aspiration and lust and arrogance that lead him to build his spire at the cost of the destruction of two men and their women. *"There is no innocent work,"* he concludes (the italics are Golding's). *"God knows where God may be."*

God may be in the lyric grace of the spire as dream, but He may also be in the spire as stone. The gossamer of the dream has to be fashioned out of heavy grey stones, each one thrusting downward on the stone beneath, and the whole sullen mass threatening to collapse. And though there has been an Annunciation, the builders are not angels; they are not even saints, but rather ordinary men who are hamstrung by their common sense and whose spirituality is muddied with lust and fear. The most spiritual of them all, Jocelin, has the same terrible ambiguity. He has answered yes to the angel's commission, and he is a dedicated priest after the order of Melchizedek; but he also finds within himself the dark depths: an obscene attraction to the red-haired Goody Pagnall, a willingness to assent to the murder of her husband, delusions of grandeur. God knows where God may be.

We are left in the end with a prose version of Yeats's "Sailing to Byzantium," in which the simple vision of the holy city is threatened by "complexities of mire and blood." Is the vision overcome? Is Jocelin a saint, giving an absolute priority to the spiritual task, or is he the desperate sinner that Roger Mason thought? Golding would surely say both. Is the spire really God's will, or is it something Jocelin has dreamed up? Is the nail he receives truly a Holy Nail, or is it any old nail, and not holy at all?

Not being a preacher, Golding does not answer these questions except to say that there is no innocent work. The disenchanted sinner who knows that all saints are frauds will point out that Jocelin deceives no one but himself. One of the last things the dying man says is "Berenice," and the saintly Father Adams thinks he means Saint Berenice. But it is more likely that the Dean was thinking of the constellation Berenice's Hair, and of Goody Pagnall's streaming hair, and of the spire as phallic symbol. God knows where God may be.

Father Adams knows of one innocent work, and he knows where God might be. His mind is plain, and with a kind of priestly profundity he resolves the ambiguity by means of a simplicity that he has known and loved. He does not know Freud, but he has known St. Paul's anxiety over the war between the law of God and the law of his members. "O wretched man that I am! who shall deliver me from the body of this death?" And Father Adams has echoed St. Paul's grateful cry, "I thank God through Jesus Christ our Lord." And so, without thinking any more about it, he lays the Host on the tongue of that tarnished splendor which is Dean Jocelin of Barchester.

The Hope of a Single Print

The literary world waits for the next Golding novel, sure only that it will have an unexpected setting. He has proven himself a master of surprise, adept at finding an unusual angle from which to view the carnival of man. *The Hot Gates and Other Occasional Pieces*, which appeared in 1966, was what the professional dancers call "a time step," meaning the deliberately undefined shuffle that marks the end of a primary passage and the pause before the next primary motion begins. The book is made up of critical essays, lectures, and autobiographical fragments, chosen from the great many reviews and occasional articles that Golding has turned out through the years. It would not have importance in its own right, had not the author been famed for his novels.

Yet there are passages in the essays that throw valuable light on his more serious work. A passage in "Islands" says that fiction is like an island that "must be built, and have an organic structure, like a tooth," and we are reminded of *Pincher Martin*. Talking about nineteenth-century space voyagers, he says, 'It is a, or rather *the,* moment of free fall—not the modern sort which can be endless, but the 19th century sort," and we think of his fourth novel.

One interesting essay on "Fable" is really a lecture that he delivered on the American Chautauqua circuit. It is especially helpful as background for *Lord of the Flies*. In it Golding makes it clear that he understands the merit and limitation of his technique, and the fact that his fables are not the traditional kind. "Perhaps in the twentieth century," he argues, "the sort of fables we must construct are not for children on any level." In these occasional pieces we notice the hand we have come to recognize: his habit of throwing some commonplace from the present into strange lights and shadows by contrasting it with some area of the past: a tourist clambers about Thermopylae and speculates about the time when the Spartans held ·the pass against Xerxes; an amateur archaeologist digs up the bones of an Iron Age woman in the path of a South Downs air strip; a child dreams that he is made an assistant to the keeper of mummies in the British Museum. All the pieces in the book, like all the novels, display Golding's special gift of animated description. The details are sharp and vivid, conveying a real world that seems to be received by our nerve endings rather than through a process of thought. He has, as V. S. Pritchett rightly observed, "an extraordinary perception of man as a physical being in a physical world."

But the pieces in *Hot Gates* show more than this sensitivity, and again they are like the novels. They show the same longing for order, the continuing search for the shape and significance of experience rather than for the anarchy of sensation. And the shape that seems to Golding always to reappear, no matter what vagaries of circumstance make the scene appear different, is the drift of man towards evil. "Man produces evil as a bee produces honey." We have been driven out of the Miltonic garden, and the angels with flaming swords bar us from returning. We have not forgotten the garden, but neither can we recapture its innocence; and even our best impulses are mixed—"knowledge of good," said Milton, "bought dear by knowing ill." This rich ambiguity provides the novels with an unfailing excitement, the consciousness of a fall into evil saving the story from sentimentality, and the consciousness of a vestigial goodness saving the book from cynicism. No matter how exotic the setting or how remote the time, we find ourselves assenting to some truth about our present world.

His existential awareness of man's predicament gives Golding's *oeuvre* its final solemnity, and gives him a distinction not widely shared in an increasingly secular world. "I am fully engaged," he rightly observed, "to the human dilemma." His characters are estranged from their own past, from nature, from their fellow men, and from God. Golding turns impatiently from any premature resolution of the human predicament—from psychology, from sociology, from Marxism, from philosophy, from religion—on the grounds that the raw experience of life cannot be categorized and hence overcome by any of man's abstractions.

Golding then joins his resonant voice to what has almost become a chorus in contemporary criticism: the belief that no continuous firmament of value is possible, and that any system of thought that pretends to be constant is without genuine ontological depth. He is afflicted by what might be called the occupational disease of poets: the notion that the creative writer does his best work in his youth, when he reacts directly and vigorously to powerful sense stimuli; and that he begins to deteriorate when his body loses its youth, and whatever structure of thought that seems most persuasive has come like a curtain to protect him from experience. This is said to have been what happened to Coleridge when he was overpowered by German idealism, to Yeats when he discovered the Rosicrucians, to Pound when he became an economist, and to Eliot when he yielded to Anglo-Catholic piety.

That there are many structures of thought from which the singular cannot extricate itself does not need to be demonstrated, nor does it need to be proved that artists are in love with singularity. Golding shares this longing for a primitive freshness of response to the tumult of a real world, and out of it comes some of his most memorable writing. But singularity is of course incommunicable, as Kierkegaard so clearly understood; and when the dance of words begins, some standard of choreography is implied. Along with Golding's artistic love of concretion is to be found the dialectical motion of his thought towards abstraction. His difficulty is that his conceptualization never seems adequate to his concretion, and that some of our age's hostility towards dogma has prevented an unashamed orthodoxy.

The Christian arrogance lies in the belief that the Faith is not a structure contrived by men to deal with the flux of experience, and so free to be accepted or discarded like Freudianism or the wave theory of light; but is rather a Truth revealed and absolute as the matrix of all lesser truths. The Christian humility lies in the belief that all human truths are tentative, and that in God's eyes no man living is justified. From the Christian viewpoint, Golding's brilliance is to be found in his true report on man's sinfulness, which is never explained as simple malice or simple seduction by society, but is always seen as both of these in addition to a strange mystery that is beyond language. There is no trace of cant in Golding's works.

But where he fails at least one believing reader is where most of the existentialists fail: he has seen so deeply the depth of the human predicament that he can invent no denouement that is equal to the plot. No ordinary resolution can rescue his protagonist from so grave a complication and permit him to live happily ever after. The great tension of his plot complication has led him to extricate his characters by means of a gimmick at the end. But what gimmick can save a man who is damned? "After such knowledge," as Eliot asked, "what forgiveness?"

The critic as believer will wonder wistfully why the answer is not obvious to Golding, as to everyone else, but appears as a shy possibility, hinted at, momentarily entertained, and then abandoned: the consolation of Israel, the faith in Beelzebub's Master who started it all and who in his good time will end it all, the lifter up of our countenance and our God. There is a possibility that Golding's great gift will develop along these lines. If it does we shall have a series of truly great novels in which the clarity and firmness of the dogma does not imperil his immediacy, but on the contrary gives the only possible metaphysical basis for the concretion on which his art depends.

SELECTED BIBLIOGRAPHY

BOOKS BY WILLIAM GOLDING

Poems. London: Macmillan, 1934; New York: Macmillan, 1935.

Lord of the Flies. London: Faber & Faber, 1954; New York: Coward-McCann, 1955.

The Inheritors. London: Faber & Faber, 1955; New York: Harcourt, Brace & World, 1962.

Pincher Martin. London: Faber & Faber, 1956; New York: Harcourt, Brace, 1957 (but with a new title, *The Two Deaths of Christopher Martin*).

The Brass Butterfly. London: Faber & Faber, 1958.

Free Fall. London: Faber & Faber, 1960; New York: Harcourt, Brace, 1960.

The Spire. London: Faber & Faber, 1964; New York: Harcourt, Brace & World, 1964.

The Hot Gates, and Other Occasional Pieces. London: Faber & Faber, 1966; New York: Harcourt, Brace & World, 1966.

ARTICLES AND BOOKS ABOUT WILLIAM GOLDING

(Essays marked with an asterisk may be found in William Nelson, ed., *William Golding's Lord of the Flies. A Source Book.* New York: The Odyssey Press, Inc., 1963.)

Amis, Kingsley, "A Man on Rockall," *Spectator,* 6698 (Nov. 9, 1956), 656.

Bowen, John, "Bending Over Backwards," *Times Literary Supplement,* 3,008 (Oct. 23, 1959), 608.*

Broes, Arthur T., "The Two Worlds of William Golding," in *Lectures on Modern Novelists,* pp. 1-14. Carnegie Series in English, No. 7 (Pittsburgh, Pa., 1963).

Cox, C. B., "Lord of the Flies," *Critical Quarterly,* 2 (Summer, 1960), 112-17.*

Davis, D. M., "Golding, the Optimist, Belies his Somber Pictures and Fiction," *National Observer,* I, 33 (Sept. 17, 1962), 17.

————, "Conversation with Golding," *New Republic,* 148 (May 4, 1963), 28-30.

Dierickx, J., "Le Theme de la chute dans les romans de W. Golding," *Études anglaises,* 16 (July-Sept., 1963), 230-42.

Drew, Philip, "Second Reading," *Cambridge Review,* 78 (Oct. 27, 1956), 79, 81, 83, 84.*

Freedman, Ralph, "The New Realism: The Fancy of William Golding," *Perspective,* 10 (Summer-Autumn, 1958), 118-28.*

Gindin, James, "Metaphor and Gimmick in the Novels of William Golding," *Modern Fiction Studies,* 6 (1960), 145-52.*

Grande, Luke M. "The Appeal of Golding," *Commonweal,* 77 (Jan. 25, 1963), 457-59.*

Green, Martin, "Distaste for the Contemporary," *Nation,* 190 (May 21, 1960), 451-54.*

Green, Peter, "The World of William Golding," *Review of English Literature,* 1 (April, 1958), 182-87.*

Gregor, Ian, and Mark Kinkead-Weekes, "The Strange Case of Mr. Golding and his Critics," *Twentieth Century,* 167 (Feb., 1960), 115-25.*

Harvey, W. J., "The Reviewing of Contemporary Fiction," *Essays in Criticism,* 8 (April, 1958), 182-87.

Herndl, George C., "Golding and Salinger: A Clear Choice," *The Wiseman Review,* 238 (Winter, 1964-5), 309-22.

Hynes, Samuel, "Novels of a Religious Man," *Commonweal,* 71 (March 18, 1960), 673-75.*

————, *William Golding.* Columbia Essays on Modern Writers, II New York: Columbia University Press, 1964.

Kermode, Frank, "Coral Islands," *The Spectator,* 201 (Aug. 22, 1958) 257.*

————, "William Golding," in *Puzzles and Epiphanies.* London: Routledge, 1962.

MacLure, Millar, "Allegories of Innocence," *Dalhousie Review,* 40 (Summer, 1960), 145-56.

Michel-Michot, Paulette, "The Myth of Innocence," *Revue des langues vivantes,* 28 (1962), 510-20.

Niemeyer, Carl, "The Coral Island Revisited," *College English,* 22 (Jan., 1961), 241-45.*

Oldsey, Bern and Stanley Weintraub, "Lord of the Flies: Beelzebub Revisited," *College English,* 25 (Nov., 1963), 90-99.

Peter, John, "The Fables of William Golding," *Kenyon Review,* 19 (Autumn, 1957), 577-92.*

Pritchett, V. S., "Secret Parables," *New Statesman,* 56 (Aug. 2, 1958) 146-47.*

Quinn, Michael, "An Unheroic Hero: William Golding's 'Pincher Martin,' " *Critical Quarterly,* 4 (Autumn, 1962), 247-56.

Rosenfield, Claire, "Men of Smaller Growth: A Psychological Analysis of William Golding's Lord of the Flies," *Literature and Psychology,* 11 (Autumn, 1961), 93-96, 99-101.*

Walters, Margaret, "Two Fabulists: Golding and Camus," *Melbourne Critical Review,* 4 (1961), 18-29.*

Young, W., "Letter from London," *Kenyon Review,* 19 (Summer, 1957), 478-82.*

M